## WHAT OTHERS SAY:

# GOD IS NO FOOL

## Lois A. Cheney

ABINGDON
NASHVILLE

**GOD IS NO FOOL**

A FESTIVAL BOOK

Copyright © 1969 by Abingdon Press

Published by Pillar Books for Abingdon Press

Festival edition published April 1977

ISBN: 0-687-15180-5

Printed in the United States of America

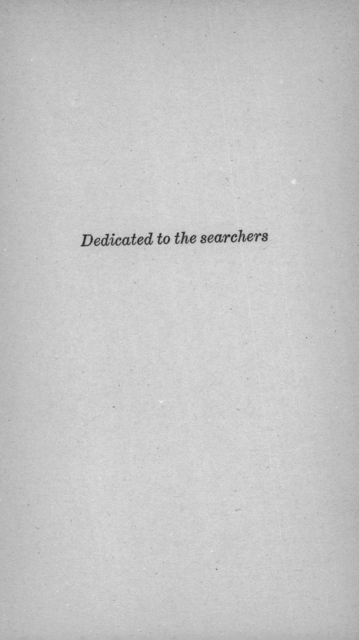

*Dedicated to the searchers*

# introduction

A daily period of time is set aside for an individual to concentrate on spiritual contact with his God, and that time is called a time of meditation, a devotional time, or simply devotions. How peculiar to call a planned patter of Bible reading, a prompted prayer, or the casual reading of someone else's thoughts, an act of devotion.

It is the premise of the thrusts on the following pages that devotion to God—the act of being devoted to his God-ness—is an act of communication. As when we communicate openly with anyone whom we love, there can be no set, static format. Exploring first one idea then another; following each urge to reflection wherever prayerful contemplation, Bible perusal, and life observation lead, they are attempts at honest encounters with God. This search began and continues in faith; faith in the all-powerful and all-loving God.

To search for the life meaning of a loving God asks much: it requires an attempt to feel, to touch, and to taste the love that is promised to those who engage in an honest reaching out to God through Christ. Thrusting from the mind and heart as a seed emerges from the ground into life, it does not try to provide tidy answers. It is just there, providing a continuing experience with Christ. It will nag throughout the days, into the nights and cut cleanly into the heart. Such has been the experience of the searchers for God throughout the ages. In our present time, when decay of meaning seeps into every life, the God who both humbled and responded to Job waits for us.

These should not be read through quickly. If they are, they will prove a disappointment. They should be pulled into yourself, argued over, thought about, prayed about, elaborated upon, diminished, or discarded—all as part of your personal search for the God who loves, the God who is no fool.

They are frequently written in the first person; it seems that almost all direct communication is.

## one

"Behold, I stand at the door, and knock; if any man hear my voice, and open the door, I will come in to him, and will sup with him, and he with me."

"Behold I stand at the door and knock."
"What door?"

"Behold I stand at the door and knock."
"What will it cost to let you in?"

"Behold I stand at the door and knock."
"Let me tidy up a bit. I'd be embarrassed to have you see things as they are here, just now."

"Behold I stand at the door and knock."
"I'll be so proud to have you come in."

"Behold I stand at the door and knock."
"It will truly be an honor, a moving experience, to have you in my humble home."

"Behold I stand at the door and knock." ...
"I want so much for you to come in."

"Behold I stand at the door and knock." . . .

     "Please, oh please, let yourself in."

"Behold I stand at the door and knock

Behold I stand . . .

Behold . . ."

## two

"And now abideth faith, hope, love, these three; but the greatest of these is love."

I heard a man say once, "I love Jesus," and
          he was a liar, and
I hated him.
I heard a man say once, "I love Jesus," and
          he was a phony.
I heard a man say once, "I love Jesus," and
          I responded to him,
"Oh yeah!"
I heard a man say once, "I love Jesus," and
          I answered, "Jesus who?"

In the silence of my room
In my heart of hearts
I murmured, "I love Jesus."

      You say it.
      The smallest verse in the Bible is,
          "Jesus wept."

# three

Once,
a man said,
"God, I can't see.
Me, I can see.
I don't know if God exists.
I *know* I exist.
God is an idea, a concept, an ex-
planation.
Me,
I have weight, height, and essence.
God contradicts himself—I don't."
Alone,
Unafraid,
Weaned from pangs of dependency,
The man stood alone,
Facing life and death,
Without excuses.

And they found the man
Standing tall
dignified
strong.
Frozen,
Quite to death.

# four

One morning I awoke with a desire I wanted to fulfill. It concerned a way I wanted to be.

This was a matter to lay before God. This was a matter for prayer. The desire was for a power and goodness, and I wanted the prayer to be right. I would preface my request with an acknowledgement of my unworthiness. This wasn't false; I knew it, and God would accept it.

All day phrases and words came to me. My special prayer took shape. I would set aside a time. I would approach him in truth.

In the evening I closed myself away from others. I read from his word. I reviewed the phrases and words of my very special prayer.

Before I got really settled down, I was flooded with the answer, and I was the way I wanted to be.

But I felt cheated . . . I had wanted that moment of communication with God. Then I thought I heard something.

"I heard you this morning."
I think I have a lot to learn about prayer.

# five

One morning I awoke with a desire I wanted to fulfill. It concerned a way I wanted to be.

This was a matter to lay before God. This was a matter for prayer. The desire was for a power and goodness, and I wanted the prayer to be right. I would preface my request with an acknowledgement of my unworthiness. This wasn't false; I knew it, and God would accept it.

All day phrases and words escaped me. My special prayer lay limp and wouldn't take shape. I would set aside a time. I would approach him in truth.

In the evening I closed myself away from others. I read from his word. I fought for phrases and words—I felt embarrassed and mute. And the world got bigger, and God got greater, and I got smaller.

Frustrated, I jerked to reality, and suddenly I was flooded with the answer, and I was the way I wanted to be.

But I felt confused . . . I had wanted

that moment of communication with God, but I had found myself impotent and alone. Then I thought I heard something.

"I heard you this morning."

I think I have a lot to learn about prayer.

# six

I had a friend; I don't think that we're friends any more. I'm not sure what happened. I missed a few of our appointed meetings. I felt sure he'd understand. A couple of times when we were talking, I saw some others approach and gave them my full attention, forgetting my friend. I felt sure that he'd understand. I didn't see him for a couple of weeks, but then when I did see him, I was careful to be enthusiastic and pretend we'd seen each other more often. He moved away. I wrote regularly for awhile, but then . . . well, you know how it is. I'm sure he knew how busy I was. I felt sure that he knew I thought of him often. I sent him a birthday card. It was a week late, but it was a funny one, and I was sure he would understand. I heard recently that he'd had some bad luck. I really felt very sorry. I'd like to send him a note, just to let him know that I care, for we were really very close, you see. As it happens, however, I can't find his address.

Last night I went to a church service, and during it we sang the old hymn, "What a friend we have in Jesus." I felt strangely embarrassed.

# seven

Something in the midst of nothing.
Nothing in the midst of something.

A mind, a body, a soul, a being.
It is born; it cries; it thinks; it dreams;
It works, and loves, and hates, and laughs,
Stumbles, fumbles, crumbles along life's
  paths.

It dies: once, twice, thrice and is gone.
Its life is swift to sunset as 'twas to dawn.
It is nothing—oh so nothing—nothing at
  all
It is a little something, only if God does
  so allow.

Something in the midst of nothing.
Nothing in the midst of something.

# eight

Who would I be?
If I were then?

Would I stand on the curb and watch him
go by? Would I have knocked off for the
afternoon to see what he had to say? Would
I have raised my eyebrows and wondered
what all the excitement was about? Would
I have stood with a few on the corner and
wondered pettishly, when *were* the authori-
ties going to put a stop to this thing before
it got out of hand! Would I have drunk it
all in, and been wide-eyed and wide-
hearted with wonder? Would I have
clinched my opinion as soon as I saw he
was associating with some of "those" kinds
of people? Would I have smiled benevo-
lently at the stories of wonders and heal-
ings? Would I have wanted to get his
autograph? Would I have stood aside and
waited thoughtfully—oh so thoughtfully—
for him to prove himself fact or fiction?
Would I have slept soundly that Friday
night, and the next night too?

Isn't it nice to be
here,
now,
for we can't make *those* mistakes.

God have mercy on us.
God have mercy on us.

# nine

If you were to paint a picture of Jesus'
   face,
What would it look like?
Especially the eyes.

I've felt eyes—
Eyes of disappointment,
Eyes of fun.

The mouth can lie,
The eyes can't.

The eyes are the windows
Of the heart.
When the heart loves,
The eyes talk.

When we pray
We get down on our knees,
We bow our heads,
We close our eyes.

We never look into the eyes of Christ.
I wonder why?
And then, again,
I think
I know why.

# ten

Is Jesus real? I mean *really* real? Did a group of men just sort of get together and decide to pull off the biggest con trick of all time? And did they write down some stories—quite alike, but not too much alike? And are they sitting on some fat cloud somewhere laughing themselves sick?

I could believe that. But what would I do with all those people who talk to me in gentleness, those with Christ twinkling in their eyes? If he didn't exist, how'd he get inside so many people? Over and over, men drop their lives and walk in Christ. Spend a day looking for Christ living in others. He's in the most unlikely people and places. If Jesus isn't real, then you're going to have to exterminate thousands who live in him.

I love it when people argue that there is no love, and then stand stupid before an act of love. I love it when people argue that there is no mercy, and then whistle and glance the other way when an act of mercy looms in front of them. I love it when people say there is no Christ, and

frown and mumble at the life that lives in
Jesus, who is stalking the world.

I wonder what people see living in
    me?
"But whom say ye that I am"?
And Simon Peter answered and said,
    "Thou art the
Christ, the Son of the living God."

"But whom say ye that I am"?

# eleven

Who was Jesus?

He was a storyteller.
He told stories. He was the world's greatest storyteller. Ask him a question; he'd
answer with a story. Give him a crowd
of people listening intently; he told them
stories. Give him an argument; he'd give
you a story. Give him a real tricky, catchy
question: he'd give you a real tricky, catchy
story.

Have you ever watched a seven-year-old
listening—inhaling—a story? Eyes wide,
mouth slung open, mind churning, he lives,
accepts, and believes. He is totally absorbed.

This man-God Jesus. He was a good storyteller. He knew what he was doing.

# twelve

Who was Jesus?
He was a wanderer.

> "The foxes have holes, and the birds
> of the air have nests; but the Son
> of Man hath not where to lay his
> head."

He knows the loneliness that has its own completeness. He wandered from his parents at the age of twelve, and they were irritated with him and were worried about him. He wandered from his home and never returned. What did his mother think? What did she think of this son who left her and her home? He wandered up and down the land, and neighbors brought her stories of his strange behavior. Did his eyes ever meet hers—hers full of quiet confusion, maybe pain? He wandered purposefully and directly to the cross, and there she had to stand quietly and watch her wandering son die.

Did she know that the cross would splinter into a million shafts that would wander through the centuries? When I wander from the good, the right, and the true; when I become discordant with my purpose; when

I wander down roads of self-pity, busyness, weakness, and pride, it is good to know that my Savior is a wanderer too. There's no place toward which I can drift, but what I'll find him there. The wanderer quietly looks at me with tired eyes filled with welcoming love.

# thirteen

Who was Jesus?
He was a very brave person.
Mark, who deals mainly with the actions
of Jesus, tells us that one day Jesus walked
through the temple. He didn't say anything, "and when he had looked round at
everything, as it was already late, he went
out to Bethany with the twelve." I don't
know what they did there, but I think
Jesus just sort of sat around and thought
a lot, and kind of got worked up. The next
time he came to the temple, he "began to
cast out them that sold and bought in the
temple, and overthrew the tables of the
moneychangers and the seats of them that
sold doves. And would not suffer that any
man should carry any vessel through the
temple." What did they do when he began
to toss things around? I like the picture of
birds flapping everywhere; money spinning
and disappearing; robes flopping around
hustling ankles.

He knew what was coming. He walked up
and into Jerusalem—just like that. A couple of nights before, he sat on a hill and
looked and looked at that city. I expect he

prayed too. He saw the whole thing coming, and he walked right into it—just like that.

The High Priest asked him "and he said unto him, Art thou the Christ, the Son of the Blessed?" And Jesus said, "I am." And when he said that, he set in motion his trial and death. According to Mark, this is the only time he actually said it. And saying it, he set up his death. He knew what he was doing.
And he did it.
And he chose to do it.
Of his own will.

## fourteen

## Crucifixus Rhythmicus

Truth slipped in
With a giant grin
On a Man's heartbeat,
And the earth glowed.

The Man stood tall
And the world smiled
With rediscovered feeling.
And the truth glowed.

Some rebuilt the man
And worshiped him
Each week at nine
With wood and rhyme.

Some molded his meaning
And to his death to hate
Caused fine additions,
And advisable conditions.

Little man monsters
Watching the fading light;
Feeble truth's heartbeat
Struggling in costly fight.

# fifteen

What is the secret of distance? It is measured in miles and years, all rather foolish. I've known the space of a few feet that had to end in "I'm sorry," to be so far, so interminably far, that the trip became impossible. I've heard a heart beat across a span of several thousands of miles, and I shook in response to its immediacy. I've seen a look of pain etched on a face in reaction to a careless cruelty. During that second of time I aged a year, ungraciously and uselessly. I've seen a glow leap from eyes receiving my love, and I was beautiful.

> Lincoln said, as he left Springfield for Washington, "Trusting in Him who can go with me, and remain with you, and be everywhere for good..."
> Matthew says that Jesus said, "Lo, I am with you alway, even unto the end of the world, Amen."
> Amen indeed!

My God, My God, how many miles! How many years do I keep between you and me? If you are with me always, why do I see you only dimly down a long, vague passage?

I would that I could walk steadily toward those I love, regardless of miles, time, and my own foolishness.

I would destroy the distance between me and the Christ.

Am I walking toward him or away from him?

# sixteen

"For truly, I say to you, if you have faith
as a grain of mustard seed, you will say to
this mountain, 'Move hence to yonder place,'
and it will move; and nothing will be impossible to you."

I've never seen a Christian move a moun-
    tain through faith.
I've never seen one so much as bend a blade
    of grass, through faith.
I've never seen such a thing.

I've heard people talk about faith.
I've heard people yearn for faith.
I've seen people with such a mustard seed
On a chain worn on their wrists, around
    their necks.

The mustard seed
Encased in a plastic ball
Was so very, very
Tiny.

God have mercy on us.
God have mercy on us.

# seventeen

Is there a hell?

Once upon a time a person was touched by God, and God gave him a priceless gift. This gift was the capacity for love. He was grateful and humble, and he knew what an extraordinary thing had happened to him. He carried it like a jewel and he walked tall and with purpose.

From time to time he would show this gift to others, and they would smile and stroke his jewel. But it seemed that they'd also dirty it up a little. Now, this was no way to treat such a precious thing, so the person built a box to protect his jewel. And he decided to show it only to those who would treat it with respect and meet it with reverent love of their own.

Even that didn't work, for some tried to break into the box. So he built a bigger, stronger box—one that no one could get into—and the man felt good. At last he was protecting the jewel as it should be. Upon occasion, when he decided that someone had earned the right to see it, he'd show it proudly. But they sometimes refused, or kind of smudged it, or just glanced at it disinterestedly.

Much time went by, and then only once in awhile would one pass by the man, the aging man; he would pat his box and say, "I have the loveliest of jewels in here." Once or twice he opened the box and offered it saying, "Look and see. I want you to." And the passerby would look, and look, and look. And then he would back away from the old man, shaking his head.

The man died, and he went to God, and he said, "You gave me a precious gift many years ago, and I've kept it safe, and it is as lovely as the day you gave it to me." And he opened the box and held it out to God. He glanced in it, and in it was a lizard—an ugly, laughing lizard.
And God walked away from him.

Yes, there is a hell.

# eighteen

"Be still and know that I am God."

The hymns rise and fall.
The organ fills and uplifts.
The choir in practiced solemnity focuses its
    praise.
Standing at the sound of prayers
        We hear the chants of Scripture fill
            the nave
            the empty, empty nave.
The sermon adds its one-voice contribution.
All, all, in reverent
Noise.

The meeting turns on Christ.
The conversation patters to Christ.
The laughter smiles with Christ.
The daily devotional drowns the Christ.
All, all, in reverent
Noise.

The first bird is heard.
The baby's cry is heard.
The pen's scratch is heard.
The embarrassed cough is heard.
Who is silent?
Who is listening to God?

Why do men run, Daddy?
Why do they always stumble and
    hurry?
To catch a bus? To get in line?
Why do they jaggle along so queer
    like?
"They stumble to din—hustling to mad-
dened murmurs
Away from the stillness; hobbling to whirl-
ing whispers,
Then past the whispers on to the shouts and
    screams!
They flee from the solid language of silence."

"Be still and know that I am God."

## nineteen

"Commit your way to the Lord;
trust in him, and he will act."
... that fool Noah did, and built a stupid
boat on dry land for years and years,
and
man lived.
... that fool Job did, and the world kicked
him, and his friends did too, and so did
his old religion, and
he showed us a new face of God.
... that fool John the Baptist did, and he
ate crunchy insects and dressed like a
jerk, and
baptized Jesus.
... that fool woman did; squeezing and el-
bowing through the crowd, just so she
could grab at Jesus with her hand, sick,
sick from years of a woman's sickness,
and
she was healed.
But now we have aptitude tests, and coun-
selors, and advisors, and rest camps, and
psychiatrists, and lots of brains, and
WE act.

"Commit your way to the Lord,
trust in him, and
he
will act."

Lord have mercy on us.
Lord have mercy on us.

# twenty

"Let the words of my mouth, and the meditation of my heart, be acceptable in thy sight, O Lord, my strength, and my redeemer."

If it were just a matter of the mouth, I wouldn't have so much trouble,

but it isn't,

and I do.

# twenty-one

The ancient Hebrews were so tied by tradition they couldn't recognize the Messiah when he was right there in front of them, and he was crucified.

The disciples, who walked and worked with the Christ, were very afraid of him; they hoped, but they also doubted, and they ran that night, and he was crucified.

The common people mobbed him, showed him their sicknesses and sores, and they threw down an aisle of palms for him and sang to him, and he was crucified.

His family was embarrassed, and stood outside, and wished he'd come home, and he was crucified.

Would we crucify Jesus today? It's not a rhetorical question for the mind to play with.
I believe,
We are each born with a body, a mind, a soul, and a handful of nails.

I believe,
When a man dies, no one has ever found
any nails left,
        clutched in his hands
                or stuffed in his pockets.

## twenty-two

My day went well,
And I thought, "God is good."

I laughed much and deeply,
And I thought, "God is good."

I worked and worked well,
And I thought, "God is good."

I read, and I understood,
And I thought, "God is good."

I offered a helping hand,
And I thought, "God is good."

I listened to uplifting music,
And I thought, "God is good."

I rested and was calm,
And I thought, "God is good."

And then,
I met God face to face,
Alone and silent.

And God sighed a deep sigh,
And my soul shook
And drove me to my knees.

God have mercy on us.
God have mercy on us.

# twenty-three

"Truly, I say to you, unless you turn and become like children, you will never enter the kingdom of heaven. Whosoever humbles himself like this child, he is the greatest in the kingdom of heaven."

"But when Jesus saw it he was indignant, and said to them, 'Let the children come to me, do not hinder them; for to such belongs the kingdom of God.'"

Once, I was in a living room; it was quiet and busy with the hum of people together. I sat listening and talking to a seven-year-old. She said, "You know what? Sometimes I think I'm tied to God. Sometimes I can feel and almost see the strings from my head and arms and legs, going right up to him." And I smiled, and the room stopped and others smiled at this little image of God's puppet. Someone said, "Isn't that cute," and we all agreed that it was cute. And the child looked up and looked around, and she smiled too, for she knew then that she'd said a cute thing.

I see the little girl frequently. She's older now. She never talks about her "strings to

heaven." But of course that's quite natural,
and as it should be;
she's growing up now,
                and grown-ups

know
better.

God forgive us.

# twenty-four

One of the exciting things about striving to become a Christian is that you never know when and where you're going to take a step closer to the Christ.

A step may take weeks, even years, and then sometimes it almost comes in an instant. Sometimes it follows devoted prayer; sometimes it follows intense meditation. Sometimes it follows a period of reverent Bible study. Other times the step follows respectful communication between Christians. But, you never really know when and where it is going to occur.

I was born with a need to laugh.
Laughter cleanses me; laughter settles me;
It stimulates me; and it fills me. I was born with a capacity for laughter.

One day, I had a "laughing" day.
Everything was a straight line ...
Every situation had its funny side ...
All day I poked, and teased, and giggled, and laughed ...
And I had to work diligently to interrupt my laughing day with periods of more serious work

        but even they got jostled with hu-
            mor,
        And I didn't care

I met laughing people that day ...
People who giggled and reacted and joked.
I looked into laughing eyes and a laughing
face,
And my heart was warmed and my soul
swelled
        both giggling as they did so.
Eventually, of course,
things calmed down;
they always do.

In the dark of night,
In the quiet of prayer,
I saw Christ—

And his eyes were red with tears,
And I felt sick,
And I looked and looked at him,
At his tear-reddened face

And I think I saw him squint
And I saw that the tears were
        tears of laughter.

And his eyes danced and twinkled,
And softly,
And almost impiously,
He chuckled.

And that night I took a step
Toward the Christ
And I loved him as I never had
Before.
And I would follow him
Anywhere!

". . . he had compassion for them, because they were . . . like sheep without a shepherd."
"The Lord is my shepherd. . . ."

Once, I was in a car, in a foreign country, and we were driving down a country road, and we came upon a flock of sheep. The shepherd moved to the side of the road, and all, *all* of the sheep followed him, regardless of whether they had to cross in front of the moving car to do so. These stupid, stupid sheep followed their shepherd without any thought at all. I've since heard that this is always true—that sheep are stupid and are easily led—and that they will follow wherever the shepherd leads, regardless of whether it leads them into danger, regardless of whether it is the sensible thing to do, even if it will kill them.

Since then, I've been very uncomfortable with the many New Testament references to the good shepherd and the fact that we are to follow God like sheep.

I live in an age that says we must rely upon

ourselves. I have been thoroughly trained and educated to take care of myself. I believe in a man taking full responsibility for his actions—walking without apology or phony humility.

As I've been trained to meet problems and essence head on—eye to eye—it is very difficult for me to bow my head. It is very hard for me to get on my knees. At times I've gotten on my knees in solitary prayer; but I wonder if my heart has ever really gotten on its knees.

He asks a great deal.
It is hard, even when you want to.

Be merciful to me, O God,
Be merciful to me,
for in thee my soul takes refuge.

## twenty-six

If I had a voice,
I'd sing to God.

If I had the hands,
I'd sculpt for God.

If I had the brains,
I'd think for God.

If I had the strength,
I'd fight for God.

If I had the skill,
I'd write for God.

If I had the faith,
I'd build for God.

If I had the heart,
I'd love for God.

If I had the money,
I'd buy for God.

And the most extraordinary thing is,
He still says, "Come."

And the most extraordinary thing is,
He commands, "Come!"
And the most extraordinary thing is,
God
and his awe-ful God-ness.

## twenty-seven

"No one born of God commits sin; for God's nature abides in him, and he cannot sin because he is born of God. By this it may be seen who are the children of God, and who are the children of the devil: whoever does not do right is not of God, nor he who does not love his brother."

Sometimes,
People argue whether there is a God or not,
Or if there is one, they then argue
Whether he's dead or not.

Sometimes,
I argue about the nature of God
Whether he's this way or that;
I wonder about the way of Christ
Whether it's this way or that.

Sometimes,
I wonder if I'll succeed,
Or if I'll do something well enough;
I wonder if I'm doing the right thing.

Sometimes,
I wonder if I'll be strong enough

Or bright enough, or good enough;
I wonder if I'll measure up.

You can't read the Bible for
More than ten minutes,
Anywhere—Old Testament or New—
Without being hit squarely with:

Some are chosen of God;
Some do not sin,
And those who sin are
Of the Devil.

And for those who sin
There is no hope,
And I am frightened
And I am small.

It isn't in keeping with the times,
This being frightened of an angry God,
But I believe in an angry God,
He can reject me . . .
            And then nothing else will matter.
            Nothing at all.

# twenty-eight

They say that God has infinite patience,
And that is a great comfort.

They say God is always there,
And that is a deep satisfaction.

They say that God will always take you
  back,
And I get lazy in that certitude.

They say that God never gives up,
And I count on that.

They say you can go away for years and
  years,
And he'll be there, waiting, when you come
  back.

They say you can make mistake after
  mistake,
And God will always forgive and forget.

They say lots of things,
These people who never read the Old
  Testament.

There comes a time,
A definite, for sure time,
When God turns around.

I don't believe God shed his skin
When Christ brought in the New Testa-
    ment;
Christ showed us a new side of God,
And it is truly wonderful.

But he didn't change God.
God remains forever and ever
And that God
is
no
fool.

# twenty-nine

They were mistaken.

Mary thought she knew her son. Mary loved and yearned for him. She followed and pleaded with him to come home. Mary wanted to protect him:
Mary was mistaken.

Peter thought he loved him most. Peter felt he knew him truly. Peter thought he would never fail his Master; Peter knew he would remain true to him no matter what happened: Peter was mistaken.

Judas thought he should organize. Judas thought he should live up to his view of the ancient promise and hope, or give it all up. Judas began to be disappointed, and he began to distrust:
Judas was mistaken.

Thomas thought they were all very gullible. Thomas loved and revered him, and Thomas missed him; he grieved at his death. Thomas didn't really believe he'd be back: Thomas was mistaken.

Now, we know his ways. Given years of scholarship and prayerful perspective, we are now ready to box and label this man from Galilee. He's ready for the completed file.

We are mistaken.

# thirty

"If any man would come after me, let him deny himself and take up his cross and follow me."

I asked some young people if they would give up and sacrifice themselves, if Christ were to call them, now, today. They were serious awhile, fidgeted, and answered awkwardly that they were tied to their homes; their parents wouldn't understand; and they felt this had to wait until they were older and could make their own decisions.

I heard a young man being asked concerning his religious convictions. He looked alternately embarrassed and irritated. He answered with long details of how active his wife was in the church; and how his kids went to Sunday school nearly every Sunday. He was relieved when his questioner left him. His eyes followed him with accusation.

I heard a young woman being asked to dedicate a portion of her time to needed Christian works. The eyebrows arched sharply and the replies came quickly in staccato rhythm. In rapid succession she listed her civic duties; her responsibilities to her children; and she concluded with reference to her husband putting his foot down about her many, too many, activities.

I heard an elderly person being asked to declare and dedicate his life in a special Christian manner. He snorted and snapped that it was the younger people's job. He'd done his work in his day, and he'd earned a rest.

The cross is a lonely place. Even Christ didn't pick it up quickly and easily.
He waits for others to do it
And he waits ...
And he waits ...

# thirty-one

One thing I have never understood is how Christians have gotten the image of being dull, uninteresting, and dedicated to lives devoid of all humor, excitement, and adventure.

The fun of being a Christian—and that is what it is—is awakening each morning with the possibility of a new step, a new enlightenment, a fresh facet of Christ burning in on us. People and things quickly become pretty predictable, but Christ—never!

I've never fully empathized with those who lean their entire faith on a few selected verses from the Bible, or on carefully chosen, regularly meeting church groups and activities. Even in the regular church service, with the regular form and the regular content, one can't stifle the inventiveness of God. From out of static, Sunday-worn monotony leaps a phrase from a song, a line from the Scripture, and the world-beat skips for us.

Often people talk about relying on Christ for the deeps of faith, hope, and peace. I do too. But the most enchanting thing that I rely upon is his ability to see through the mist of my insufficiency and awkwardness, spot the moment that is right, and spring a new lock that flings open the door to a fresh vista.

Sometimes it comes when I'm alone. Sometimes when I'm listening to another. Sometimes at work. I've even wakened out of a sound sleep from a tap of Christ. Sometimes I see it; other times I hear it, or feel it. Always it makes me smile.

It must be very dull not to be a searching Christian, and never know the surprise of Christ.

# thirty-two

You can measure greatness by medals and ribbons. You can measure a man's stature by the number of pages written about him. So doing you feel your own smallness becoming even smaller. You lie in an atmosphere of do-lessness and nothingness—basking lazily in the silhouettes of the great ones.

There is a small greatness that is asked of each of us. Each is capable of greatness in his vocation, in his personality, in his character. There are still pools of greatness within us waiting to be challenged, to be beckoned. The worship of the great ones is wrong if it keeps us from developing our own greatness, however small.

Could the call from Christ be the call to our own small greatness?

# thirty-three

Once upon a time,
God sighed a great sigh . . .
He watched what a mess man was making
of his manhood. Men in their insatiable
search and fear were running around and
worshiping stones, and trees, and thunder,
and the sun, and fertility, and harvest time
. . . and many other things.

> And God had pity, and he touched a
> man, and therefore a whole nation
> of people, and he said rather blunt-
> ly, "I am the Lord your God." And
> a new age was born, for God was
> one, and God was all.

Once upon a time,
God sighed a great sigh . . .
He watched what a mess man was making
of his manhood. Men, even the chosen
ones, were encasing him in a body of laws
and rules and rituals and procedures and
hollow pomp. Men had taken the idea of
a just and only God and twisted it, and
they had begun to wander in and out of
faith and non-faith.

> And God had pity, and he looked
> around and decided on that which

meant the very most to him, and Jesus was born on earth. And a new age was created. Laws evolved into love; and judgment expanded into mercy; and fear dissolved before grace.

Once upon a time,
God sighed a great sigh . . .
He watched what a mess man was making of his manhood. Men had fought over the Jesus; they had entombed him in procedure, in ritual, and had buried him in restrictions. And men, in their insatiable fear and search, ran around and worshiped numbers and nature and their own minds and power . . . and many other things.

Once upon a time . . .

# thirty-four

"Truly, I say to you, unless you turn and become like children, you will never enter the kingdom of heaven."

I guess the worst thing about growing up is that fun and amazement drift into sporadic entertainment and forced, ritualized behavior. The glow of vocation slips into the monotony of procedure. The exhaustion that comes from playing too hard becomes more effort than it is worth. Comfort is more yearned for than the experience of reading or talking away the night. Joy becomes a matter of observing and reflecting on the almost grotesquely carefree child.

Christ spoke several times of children and of his attraction to them. He thought we needed to be like them, in some ways.

I pray that I never mistake atrophy of imagination for maturity. I pray that I never approach Christ so solemnly and so full of the cynicism of years and doubts that I find him distracted while I whine to him. I pray I never see his eyes wander from me as he searches for a child lost in play.

# thirty-five

I once knew a man who had been given a very special gift. In his particular field he had the heart and ability of an artist. And more impressive was that this art was dedicated to its giver, Christ. As this man's life unfolded, so did his gift, and he seemed very special in the eyes of God and man.

He became deeply concerned with the problems of those about him. Little by little he became less an artist and more a servant to those about him. He did it well, and they loved him, and worked him, and used him, and fastened on him with a death grip. Several times in his life fresh thrusts were made to reopen the door to his art, and each time, after careful contemplation, he would close the door and turn back to the worried eyes of those about him.

The man is a fine man, and one whom I'm sure will one day face God, in truth. I'm sure that God will reach his hand out to him and accept him. But I wonder if God's eyes might also flicker in disappointment.

When Christ talks to us about not

being conformed to this world, I think he means more than just avoiding evil and wickedness. I think he means keeping our eyes on him and using our very special gifts from him, as *he* intended, not as the world whispers. The choice is not always clear . . . it is a tightrope decision, and one way will lead closer to Christ than the other.

## thirty-six

I know a pain,
That passeth all understanding
And when I feel that pain,
I understand it.

I know a truth
That defies all understanding
And when I live that truth
I understand it.

I know a love
That passeth all understanding
And when I feel that love
I understand it.

I know a God
That passeth all understanding
And when I love that God
I understand him.

# thirty-seven

"... and, lo, I am with you alway, even unto the end of the world."

Did you ever wonder what you would do in the time of crisis? Days pass into months of seemingly endless safety, but there always lurks the sudden pain, the sudden grief, the unexpected interruption that jerks life from its normal path.

I've watched some face the chasms of life and fail. I've watched others face them and walk confidently across.

As a Christian I feel a special obligation to face life. But I've long wondered whether my faith would be strong enough; whether my courage would be broad enough; and whether I would be able, alone, to meet the challenge.

And one time, it came like a dawning. The Christ seemed to angrily remind me that a Christian never faces anything alone. The great promise of Christ is to be there, with his hand on our shoulders.

We do not face life alone.

# thirty-eight

One day,
Just one day.

If I could present to my God,
Just one day
of pure intention
of faithful purpose
of loving heart
of prayerful actions.

Just one day,
of total commitment
of untarnished speech
of unselfish acts
of total concentration.

Just one day,
lacking weakness
lacking jealousy
lacking self-absorption
lacking foolishness.

Just one day,
One day
If I could present to my God,
Just one day.

## thirty-nine

Hey! look at us
We're digging and digging
Into stubborn, ancient earth;
We're discovering
Where we came from,
and how we came.

"but where are you going?"

Hey! Look at us
We're learning and learning
Into stubborn laws
Of nature and space
And non-nature and non-space;
We're discovering
All there is to know.

"but where are you going?"

Hey! look at us
We're planning and planning
Into stubborn years
Of education and training
And hopes and dreams;
We're discovering
How not to waste any time.

but where are you going?"

Hey! look at us
We're shiny and bright
And clever and sophisticated
And witty and well-read;
We're discovering
How to really fill up
This old life.

"but where are you going?"

where?

"Yes; where?"

# forty

Who is God?

The name of God—that which he called himself was "I am."

And man searches a lifetime trying to discover his "I am." Like the tightly closed flower, it resists the attempts to peel down, petal by petal, superfluous meaning leading to the discovery of his pure, white core.

Men write poems probing the essence of the purposelessness that kills. Men spend a lifetime running after this meaning. Believing and hoping, filled with doubt, they seek. Men drink and love and hate and sleep in search of and in defiance of this "I am."

The high school senior, the college sophomore, the sedentary adult, all strain to the eternal question, "Who am I?"

To stand quietly in perfect perspective with the world and the non-world, and to say "I am" is to be God.

To strive for purity of purpose. To smother strife in gentleness; to keep open and receptive to life in all its life-giving and life-denying aspects, is to strive to be God-like.

# forty-one

"So faith, hope, love abide, these three; but the greatest of these is love."

Love has many gentle faces.

Once, I watched six people coming out of a house to enter a car. The young father strode with lazy purposefulness and nonchalant strength carrying a wheelchair folded up in one hand. He moved to the car and stood holding the door open. A young boy burst out of the house and exploded down the stairs, arriving at the car after a swift, circuitous route that examined every step of the yard, the walk and the nearby road. Then he stood, patient in his impatience opening and closing another of the car's doors, in careless enjoyment. Another child skipped, ran, and jumped in a direct path to the car. Once there she snatched the wheel chair which was leaning against the car. She lunged into it after first jerking it open. She wheeled it in tight little circles first in one direction and then another; then streaked down the sidewalk, jammed to a stop, whirled around and tore back to the car, all midst her own chorus of sounds and whoops. The young mother had followed between husband and children, glancing at each of them in turn, wrapping them in care, love, and easy acceptance. Then she looked back at the house with the same kind of care. Emerging slowly from the door now came an old man, slight of build, weak but not frail, cautious but not unsure. He had his arms around an old woman, who was apparently his wife. She was weak and frail, cautious and unsure. Shuffling slowly, guided by an arm of love at her back, and a hand of love covering one of her own, she made her way slowly to the waiting car, waiting man, waiting woman, waiting children, and waiting wheelchair.

All this took about five minutes, and I felt I had watched more love and more strength and more acceptance than I'd ever read or studied about. It was a scene of life, encased in love in all its many forms.

Every face in this group wore a smile—
some easier and more casual than others.
And I smiled constantly the rest of the
evening, and I felt good. And I think God
smiled too.

# forty-two

They say Abraham was a friend of God—
"Abraham, the friend forever," said God.

A friend touches the anger, the fear, the
pain, the secret yearnings with acceptance.

A friend listens and listens to the words
and the lack of words with acceptance.

A friend laughs with, not at. A friend
weeps with and for, all in deep acceptance.

A friend walks away with the full assurance
it is the same as walking toward.

A friend lets you walk away, and you have
the assurance you may return.

A friend demands all you have with the
faith it is the same thing as giving all he
has.

A friend gives all he has with the conviction it is the same as receiving all you have.

A friend speaks freely, yet gently.

> It is good—in the magnificent sense
> —to know that God would be a
> friend to a man. I know of no reli-
> gion in which the God is both God
> and friend. We fear him because he
> is all-powerful. We worship him be-

cause he is all goodness. We bow in humility before him because he is all master. We serve him because he is all-purposeful. But perhaps the most significant thing of all is that we love him, because he is a friend forever.

# forty-three

Bits and pieces
Bits and pieces

People. People important to you, people un-
important to you cross your life, touch it
with love and carelessness and move on.
There are people who leave you and you
breathe a sigh of relief and wonder why
you ever came into contact with them. There
are people who leave you and you breathe
a sigh of remorse and wonder why they
had to go away and leave such a gaping
hole. Children leave parents; friends leave
friends. Acquaintances move on. People
change homes. People grow apart. Enemies
hate and move on. Friends love and move on.
You think on the many who have moved
into your hazy memory. You look on those
present and wonder.

I believe in God's master plan in lives. He
moves people in and out of each other's
lives, and each leaves his mark on the other.
You find you are made up of bits and pieces
of all who ever touched your life, and you
are more because of it, and you would be

less if they had not touched you.

Pray God that you accept the bits and pieces in humility and wonder, and never question, and never regret.

Bits and pieces
Bits and pieces

# forty-four

The pain of pain is disappointment, for it cannot be taped or healed or cut away. Dull, creeping out of nowhere, it settles and seeps, covering heart, mind, and perspective.

The task that loomed as special, glowing with promise and challenge, slips into meaninglessness. The task aimed at, sought for, planned on, arrives; and what glowed is tarnished, and what beckoned seems hollow. And disappointment smothers.

The eyes that loomed as special, glowing with warmth and shared moments, slip into the sea of uncaring eyes. Moments awaited, arrive; and untrue words rattle aimlessly around the room. What seemed real now appears false; what appeared expansive now narrows. And disappointment smothers.

One could become angry and feel cheated in the disappointments that move into hopes, dreams, and daily steps. One could turn hard, cold—except for two questions. How many times do others watch me in dull disappointment? How often do the eyes of Christ look on, throbbing in disappointment?

God have mercy on us.

# forty-five

I believe
that Meditation is a lost art.

They talk about meditation
in the Old Testament
some.

They talk about meditation
in the New Testament
a little.

They talk about meditation
in the present time
not at all.

Today,
we have all kinds of
other things
to do.

We sing and pray and listen
in God's house,
together.

We worship and fear and love
in God's house
together.

We think and talk and worry
in lots of houses
together.

We feel good and bad and so-so
in lots of houses
together.

I wonder, if he wanted to,
if he really, really
wanted to

Whether he could be heard
what with all the
singing
and praying
and talking
and feeling good
and feeling bad
and feeling so-so.

I think God talks
in whispers,
in tiny
little
whispers,

And to hear a tiny
little whisper, you
must be very, very
silent,
and very, very
alone,
and open.

And that is what
I believe
meditation
is.

And it is a lost art
And that makes
God
a lost art.

But, I believe
that somewhere
he whispers,
waiting for someone
to
meditate
and hear.

# forty-six

I once watched a boy pretend he was a man. He looked cross and sober; he deliberately slowed and lowered his voice. He walked in mock dignity; he spoke in unpracticed profundity. He spoke of God and man and life and truth. He'd dressed like the man he would be, not like the boy he was. All went well until he giggled, and then his friends giggled and the pretend was over.

I once watched a man pretend he was a Christian. He was cross and sober; his voice was deep and deliberate. He walked in dignity; he spoke in practiced profundity. He spoke of God and man and life and truth. He dressed like the man he would be, not like the man he was. All went well until he giggled, and then his friends giggled and the pretend was over.

Sometimes,
I'm not at all certain
That God has a sense of humor.

## forty-seven

Today,
    For what I am that I ought not to be,
    Forgive me.
    For what I am not that I ought to be,
    Forgive me.

    Be with my mouth in what it speaks.
    Be with my hands in what they do.
    Be with my mind in what it thinks.
    Be with my heart in what it feels.

    Work in me
      through me
      for me
      in spite of me.

# forty-eight

"And he answering said, Thou shalt love the Lord thy God with all thy heart, and with all thy soul, and with all thy strength, and with all thy mind."

How much money do I have to give to the church to be a good Christian?

> There was one I loved, and it came time to buy a gift. What I wanted to give cost too much and was out of the question. But I saved, and went without, and bought the gift, and I was deeply happy.

How much time do I have to give to the church to be a good Christian?

> There was one I loved, and I dreaded our separations. And we planned and devised ways to find time to be together; to talk together; to work together; to laugh together. And when we were together, I lost track of time, and I was deeply happy.

How much of my behavior do I have to have regulated by God in order to be a good Christian?

There was one I loved, and I wanted his respect. I was careful with my language; careful in my work. I lived as truly as I could, so he would nod his head in approval. With him or away from him, I acted in a way I thought he would admire. And as I strove thus to be more than myself, I was deeply happy.

God,
Forgive us.

# forty-nine

I once knew a young man who was searching for God. And I was touched by his search; and I prayed for his search; and I loved his search.

He read a lot of books. He thought and thought about their ideas. He talked to many people, in pairs and in groups; they matched their minds with his and they furthered his search. He walked and sought God in the rain. He climbed and sought God on the mountain. He closed himself off from the world and sought God in his soul.

He would describe his searchings and travels for truth. He would explain how he had meticulously and prayerfully sorted, rejected, and accepted.

As the years went on, I changed from anticipating the recountings of his searches, to simply receiving them; to being bored with them; to avoiding them; and him. You see, he had fallen in love with his search.

God just isn't that hard to find.

## fifty

Once I saw a little boy proudly show his mother a painting he'd made at school. She looked at it, and turned it this way and that, and looked some more. "It's lovely, just lovely," she murmured. Suddenly, she exclaimed, "Oh! I see what it is! It's a house and a tree, and there's a big sun, and . . ." The little boy grabbed the paper and bunching it all up, he hollered, THAT'S NOT WHAT IT MEANT!

Did you ever, oh so carefully, lay out just how things were, and how they worked, and why they worked, and then sat back satisfied? Then you heard someone repeat what you'd said, oh so carefully, and you hardly recognized it, and your brain screamed.
THAT'S NOT WHAT I MEANT!

Did you ever pry out of your heart, your mind, a tiny nugget of how you truly felt, and then told someone, probably someone special, and then stared in disbelief as

he responded wrong, all wrong, and your
every pore shouted,
THAT'S NOT WHAT I MEANT!

Sometimes, smug times
When I'm talking about God
When I'm praying about God
When I'm working for God,

Sometimes, smug times
When I'm very busy
in the church
about the church
around the church
I wonder
if God isn't
sighing,
or whispering,
or saying,
or hollering,
THAT'S NOT WHAT I MEANT!

## fifty-one

Before the battle a soldier said, "I am afraid." In that battle he performed beyond himself.

Before a certain, important sermon a minister said, "I am afraid." In that sermon he preached better than he was able.

Before an overwhelming challenge Moses said, "I am afraid." From that challenge came the future of God's people.

It's old-fashioned to have fear.

We don't have to fear God any more,
                    —grin and wink—
The ole guy just rolled over and died.

We don't have to fear sin any more,
                    —grin and wink—
We just label the response and alter the stimulus.

We don't have to fear hell anymore,
                    —grin and wink—
It is just a medieval myth.

We don't have to fear anything any more,
                    —grin and wink—

We can use it, dissolve it, or absorb it.

Man-giants, it would seem
Knew when to fear

Where,
Oh where
Are the Christian giants?
—grin and wink—

# fifty-two

There comes a time
When you accept the fact
That you will not face God
With a diamond in your hands.
He will forgive you.

But,
If there comes a time
When you face your God
With nothing in your hands,
He will not forgive you.

He who has ears,
Let him hear.

# fifty-three

There was a place
Where the unbelief was so great
That Jesus
Jesus, the Son of God,
Could not heal and help
And so he left them.

Has anyone seen Jesus lately?

## fifty-four

Once
A long time ago
God spoke to a man
And the ground around the place where God
was speaking was so holy that he made the
man take off his shoes, just to stand there.

Once,
When God's house was new,
Only certain very special and very holy
people were allowed into its center, where
God himself lived for it was so holy.

Once,
When they were carrying God's house
From one place to another, one of the holi-
est parts, the part that held God's very
words, slipped, and a man
(he only wanted to help)
reached out to keep it from falling, and
God struck him dead,
for it was so very holy.

And
This holy God
From time to time,
a long time ago,

talked right out to certain holy men
like Abraham,
      and Moses,
          and David,
             and others.

Today,
We have crosses for earrings
And crosses for necklaces
And wallet size pictures
of Jesus
in living color.

We have little saints
for our cars;
And we sometimes
start important
football games
and baseball games
with
little
prayers.

And the God
the Holy God
who spoke to a certain few,
a long time ago,
talks right out
to no one ...
anymore,
as far as I know.

God have mercy on us.

## fifty-five

I once saw a cross so big
It was as high as the church
In front of which it stood.
It was made of railroad steel
And it was very dramatic,
And I was moved
And I was impressed
As I walked by and away from it.

I once saw a cross so lovely,
It was a work of art,
Carved and polished
It was made to look
Both strong and delicate,
And I was moved
And I was impressed
As I walked by and away from it.

There once was a cross
Not so high; not so lovely
It was not a work of art.
Rough, full of splinters
Uneven, unsymmetrical
Its simple mystery
Unfathomable.
And I cannot walk by it
And I cannot walk away from it.

## fifty-six

I live where I hear trains. That's good. The night sound of trains surrounds my most quiet and intimate moments. Perhaps each person has a lonely sound with which he has grown up—cars echoing up and down the highway in front of his home; a pine tree murmuring its secrets; a bus laboring, snorting, wheezing its lonely paths; the low mumble of voices in another part of the house. You grow up listening and drifting on the sound. The sound becomes tangled in memories and wonderings and getting older and fears and doubts.

I heard trains as I prayed "Who am I?"

I listened to trains as a loved one left.

I heard trains when life turned into death in a person of my heart.

I hear trains when there is self-doubt.

I hear trains when my mind and imagination drift and wander.

I hear trains when I whisper "Forgive me."

What was the sound in your life?

What was it you listened to the sleepless nights as you dreamed beyond your home and family? Where did you spend that night? and what sounds kept you awake that night—that night you ran away from your parents, the night before you spent the day in the temple asking questions? What did you hear after that strange, wild-looking man baptized you? What sounds did you hear when you wandered alone out on the mysterious desert? You liked the sea; was it the lonely wash of water on small beach pebbles you heard? You often climbed hills; was it the sound of wind swirling its lonely stillness? When you crossed the Kidron and spent much of that night in prayer, what lonely earth sound kept you company? High on that cross; when all seemed lost and for nothing; when your lonely cry pierced God's turned back— "Why hast thou forsaken me?"—what did you hear? What did you listen to, those lonely, awful hours?

When I hear trains
And it is quiet
And I am alone

I think of Jesus
And he seems very, very real to me
And it is good when Jesus is real
When he is more than books
        and thoughts
        and hymns
        and prayers
I think I could reach out and touch him.
And I know he can reach out and touch
   me.

## fifty-seven

I stand before the cross
and wonder.

I stand before the cross
and fear.

I kneel before the cross
and weep.

I pray before the cross
and rejoice.

To know the cross
Is to know Christ.

To feel the cross
Is to feel Christ.

To gaze at the cross
Is to gaze at Christ.

To carry the cross
Is to be a Christian,
And not until then.

God, forgive us.

## fifty-eight

I gave an hour to God,
And in that hour, his peace poured out
and made me able for many, many hours.

I gave some money to God,
And through that money, I felt touched
by others I didn't know, but who had a
    need.

I gave a morning to God,
And in that time his music, his words, his
    strength
flowed in and over, and
I was more.

I gave some thought to God,
And in that thought, he prodded and com-
    forted,
and my thoughts were more than they
    could be.

I gave a prayer to God,
And in that prayer, he reached out and
    touched me,
and I rose up, taller than I had been.

And I looked at my giving
and it was all taking,
And I bowed before my God.

And I bowed before my God.
And I bowed before my God.

# fifty-nine

Thank God.

Thank God for those who see into us, through us, and to the self that is beyond ourselves. There have been those few who refused our superficial roles, who have seen beyond our clever chatter; who have waited beyond our preoccupation. Reaching through our facades, which we have very carefully built, they have seen a beauty which we all have, but which, for most of us lies buried deep inside. The beauty was planted there by God. He then touches those few, who through love, touch us. Much of the positive which we do and think is in response to those who have smiled past the shell into the white light. Thank God and thank them, and pray we never stop trying to measure up to what he and they believe we can be.

## sixty

If someone were to steal my Bible,
If I were to be barred from church,
If those I share my God with were to leave
    me,
If the hymns were to be denied me,
If the God-inspired, man-wrought creeds
    were to vanish,

If all these deeply meaningful, but outside
    forces were to go,

Could God still get through to me?
Would I still see and feel my God?

My God, My God
Have mercy on me.

## sixty-one

There are those who reach out and touch us in their need. There is the God who opens us to another's needs and this is the crisis of Christian responsibility. We perceive it; we waken to it; and we yearn to fulfill it. The danger of the blunder, the misstep is as close as the glow of fulfillment. When the moment arrives we must act in deep, yearning prayer. It is at these moments when God works most surely through us. It is so frightening that many turn away, afraid of the slash on soul and ego. For those who do not turn away, God blesses, promising nothing, but hoping as deeply as we hope.

When we have grown past praying for personal peace,
When we have matured past praying for comfort,
When we have moved past praying for self,
When we move into praying for strength to act,
I think we are then making the most important prayer there is.

# sixty-two

I awoke one morning and found that I could think of very few of the people for whom I cared who were not isolated in pain. One wept through fresh and slashing grief. One stared at a clay form that would have been life. One shuffled through days of loneliness, emptied of the one love that had shared years of days with him. Another fumbled through the monotony of daily chores, feeling purposelessness. Another mutely performed the tasks of many years, shackled with feelings of failure and disappointment. Two others walked, day by day, paths surrounded by pain and imminent death that hovers over their shoulders.

And I wept because I could not touch, speak, or hold off the pain they felt, for all pain is in isolation. And I knelt in my soul of souls, and committed them to the velvet-steel arms of the Christ who cares.

And that day I walked in sadness, but confident in the caring Christ, and I felt flooded in all-love.

I know why I am a Christian.

# sixty-three

Today I watched people walking—walking together—boys walking together; girls walking together; boys and girls walking together. They were most together when they matched strides. Adjusting to one another they took on a secluded world as they strolled, hustled, or meandered, step for step—something touching, more often not. It seemed that, of necessity, if they were walking together, they must also be matching thoughts, talk, and themselves. Each movement was unconsciously synchronized in rhythm. It made those walking alone seem so alone. Those walking with others, but out of step, seemed so apart.

We speak of walking with God and talking with God and being with God. Can you imagine truly striding with God? You'd find his steps matching yours, and matching your thoughts, your purposes, your dreams, and for those moments you'd be so completely together.

I want to walk with God.

## sixty-four

Today, I made a joke about God,
And many laughed.
And I felt clever.

Today, I was blunt about God,
And many smirked,
And I felt clever.

Today, I was crude about God,
And many responded,
And I felt clever.

Today, I threw out God,
And many were glad,
And I felt clever.

Today, I forgot all about God,
And no one cared,
And I felt clever.

Tonight, I talked to God,
And he turned his back.
And I was cursed
      and
        alone.
My God.
My God.

## sixty-five

Once upon a time
There was a God
Who so loved the world
That he gave his son
His only son.

And they took that son
And they hung him on a cross
And that son died
And they buried the son—
Sealed him up tight.

But God said,
"Oh no you don't"
And he rolled back the rock
He unsealed his son
And his son came out
Came out walking and breathing
And he was Alive.

And he's alive today
And he walks around
And he stalks around
Breathing life and life
Every morning, just before dawn
For thousands of years
Little grim people—
Preachers and bankers and
Storekeepers and students—

Sneak up to the grave and
Roll back the stone
To seal it up tight.

And every morning
God roars
"Oh no you don't!"
And he flings back
the stone.

And out walks Jesus
All over again;
Out stalks the
Grinning, striding
Jesus.

Tight-lipped
Little people
Hover all day
Around the tomb
And cover it with
Incense
And bow before it
And walk before it
And sigh before it;
And pray to it
And sing to it

And weep to it
And lean on it.

And no one
Notices
Or at least
They pretend not
To notice,

The living
Breathing
Walking
Talking
Jesus

Out on the
Edge, calling
"Hey!"
"Hey you!"

## sixty-six

Suppose,
That every day,
the Christ, the living, breathing Jesus
Walked through every town
Every single town

And no one ever saw him
Because they were
In church, or
In bed, or
At work, or
At breakfast, or
In school, or

Going some place,
Or standing still,
Or coming from somewhere,
Or running to catch something,
Or lagging to avoid something

Or in their cars,
Or at their hairdressers,
Or at the store,
Or at the cleaners,
Or at the gas station
Or doing dishes,
Or mopping the floor,

Or reading a book,
Or listening to a lecture,
Or taking a nap,

While Christ just
walked through every town
Every single town.

I'll bet he chuckled
when he did that
several thousand years ago,
But I'll bet
the joke's gone stale
And I'll bet he doesn't
chuckle about it
anymore;
As he goes through every town,
Every single town.

## sixty-seven

This is a Christian
Look at the Christian
See the Christian pray.
Pray, Christian, pray.

This is the church
Look at the church
Hear the church bells.
Ring, bells, ring.

This is the book
Look at the book
Read all the truth.
Speak, truth, speak.

This is the cross
Look at the cross
"Oh" to the cross.
"Oh," cross, "Oh."

There is the God
Look at the God
Why does he Weep?
Weep, God, Weep.

## sixty-eight

A woman came from seeing a religious movie. She was moved by it. She thought of the technicolor wonders of God. She choked up at the vista-vision close-up of the men of God. She mused on the stereophonic destruction of evil. All the way home she thought and thought. When she had gotten dinner, she bathed the children, played bridge, and then went to bed. Before she fell asleep, she told her husband about the movie, and said, "It really made you think."

A young man went into a church after a long, too long, absence. The minister spoke of the Love of God, of the Hope of God, of Life in God. The young man was troubled and he was stirred. That afternoon, he went for a walk with his girlfriend, and they talked, and they had a hamburger. Before he kissed her goodnight, he told her about the sermon, and he said, "It really made you think."

A grown man concerned for life and love read many books of religious depth. They spoke of the Need for God, the Hope for God, and the Promises of God. He

couldn't put them down. He would read late into the night. At breakfast he would tell his wife why he had stayed up so late. He would tell her about a special book, and would say,
"It really made you think."

Could it be
That the loneliest book in the Bible
Is the book
"The Acts"?

## sixty-nine

People die every day. People hurt every day. I read about their deaths, their tragedies in the paper, as I eat supper. I hear about their pain on the radio, as I dress in the morning. I keep up to date on the grief of the world. I am informed.

A look of disappointment flitted across the face of one I cared for, and my breath came quicker. All day I could not get that look from my mind. Before I slept that night, I tried to erase that look, and then I prayed for it, and then I fell asleep, troubled.

Does God love us so much?
Does he see and feel every glance?
Does he think about it all day?
Surely not!
Surely not the Great God
Who rules the seas and the wind
Who has witnessed stupidity and pain
For century upon century.

And yet
I think he does:
And the force of that thought
smothers me.

## seventy

Once,
A boy cheated on a test.
He got a good grade on the test,
And passed the course.
He told his friends
"I had no choice."

Later,
As a man he took a job
that denied another need
but the money was good
and he had his family to think of,
And he told a friend,
"I had no choice."

Later,
The man denied his calling
And chose a different role
And it made him quite famous
And he became well thought of,
He told a friend,
"I had no choice."

Later,
The man reviewed his life
before God, the Almighty God.
He shrugged his shoulders

as he told God,
"I had no choice."

And God said
as he turned his back
and walked away from
the astonished man
"I have no choice."

## seventy-one

Once, I prayed,
Who am I?

If only I knew who I was.
If only I knew what I could do.
If only I knew why I was.
If only I knew what to do.

And I prayed more earnestly,
Who am I?

If only I knew, faith would come.
If only I knew, strength would spread.
If only I knew, I could
work and serve and grow.

And I demanded in prayer
Who am I?

And he smiled,
And said,
"It is enough that I know,
Follow me."

And I did.

## seventy-two

Once, a little boy said,
"Where is God?"
And his mother said,
"Eat your lunch."

And he grew older.

And he asked a teacher,
"Where is God?"
And the teacher said,
"Do your homework."

And he grew older.

And he asked a minister,
"Where is God?"
And the minister said,
"Go to church."

And he grew older.

He ate his lunches
And he did his homework
And he went to church.

And pretty soon,
He didn't ask anymore
"Where is God?"

# seventy-three

How does God's truth prevail?

A large chunk of truth was placed right in the midst of men by the Almighty God. And men saw it and were awed by it, and were humbled by it. They walked around and around it, looking at it, gazing at it, and loving it. Then they got organized. First, they posted a guard over it, while others built a fortress for it. That was o.k. for awhile. Then they decided to do more with it. So they sent in five wise, devout men to study it. They stayed in there a long, long time. Then strange and quarrelsome noises began to come from within the fortress, and out stalked the five men, red-faced and very angry, each with a large packet of papers under his arm. They walked off in five different directions reading loudly from their papers, which said what the chunk of truth really meant. People scurried around, first listening to one and then another, and finally they grabbed up their belongings and followed after the one they liked the best. And they built little camps about a mile away and studied the pages of their chosen leader, which told them what the truth really meant.

Things would be calm for awhile, then from first one camp and then another, would come sounds of angry voices and scuffling. And you'd see several people jump up and walk off in different directions with fresh packets of paper under their arms, that explained what the truth really meant. Again, little clusters of people would follow, and they'd establish fresh camps about a mile further off. This went on and on.

Soon there were many, many camps for miles and miles in all directions, each with its packet of papers, explaining how the truth really was. Sometimes they would argue and debate which of them was closer to the ancient fortress. Sometimes there'd be awful fights between camps, and the camp that won would proudly enlarge its scope of what truth really meant, and pride themselves on expanding and perpetuating the real truth. Sometimes camps would combine their packets of paper. Sometimes, some people would get weary with the whole thing, and go off without any papers at all. They'd establish camps where the land was good or the water was plentiful or some other reason that certainly seemed more reasonable than setting up a camp around some silly papers.

Every once in awhile would come a wanderer, usually all alone. He would wander through the camps or skirt them, and would wind up coming right up to the neglected and overgrown fortress, and walk right in and stare at the real chunk of truth. He would gaze and gaze at it, and pick it up and handle it, and stroke it, and then set it down and walk right out and start strutting all over the place, glowing and carrying on, and generally throwing camps into confusion. He would do all sorts of old-fashioned things in old-fashioned ways, grinning and humming all the while he did it.

And *that's* how God's truth prevails.

## seventy-four

Moses said, "Oh Come on now! Be sensible! Not me! I'm a terrible speaker. They'd never listen to me." And God said, "Oh, for crying out loud! O.K., I'll use your brother to help with the speaking." And Moses led God's people out of disintegration.

Jonah said, "Oh Come on now! Be sensible! Not me! I'm not the type." And after a rather unexpected vacation in a fish, just thinking things over, he talked to God's people, and led them God's way.

And Zacharias said, "Oh Come on now! Be sensible! Not me! My wife and I are too old to have any kids." And God said, "Oh shut up!" And he did shut up—for nine months. And John was born, and the way for the Christ opened up.

And I heard a child say,
"I can't serve God, I'm too young."

And I heard a boy say,
"I can't serve God, I'm not good
enough."

And I heard a woman say,
"I can't serve God, I'm not skilled
enough."

I wonder if God ever gets any new problems.

## seventy-five

Once,
A man
A very good man
decided he was really going to sell God. He felt that what was missing was that God had been encrusted with old-fashioned language, outdated appeal, and outmoded presentation.

Using all his skill and imagination, which were considerable, he devised a meeting to make his pitch. First, he converted the God message to modern terms. Then, he constructed a backdrop of modern, catchy, art abstractions. He chose a variety of throbbing, up-to-date folk music to sustain the mood. Keeping the atmosphere light and comfortable, he had his audience sit casually and easily. No special dress was required, and he came casually dressed also. He talked, chatted, joked, and just generally conversed with people about the meeting. The music set the mood; the special lighting worked dramatic hues and focuses on the abstract background.

Afterwards, he was complimented on the creativeness, the stirring mood, the timely approach. He was pleased and comforted, and said that he was glad that they liked it, and then added chuckling, that he hoped they'd buy his product. People looked confused and uncomfortable, and finally someone said,
"Oh! you selling something?"

## seventy-six

Once,
A long, long time ago,
A very special group of people, chosen by God, witnessed many of his miracles and received many of his special favors. But they grew impatient and got critical, and because of their lack of faith, he let them wander and wander in a hot, barren wilderness, and a whole generation of them died off.

Once,
A long time ago,
A very special group of people, chosen by God, grew impatient and lax in their attention to him, and he hurled enemies at them who slaughtered them and destroyed their homes and temple, and drove them to a strange land, and they were without home or peace.

Not so long ago,
A large group of people grew impatient with God, and they turned their attention to themselves and their own minds, and what they could contrive all by themselves. And they could contrive many wonderful

things. And then they had a war. And they spread poison over each other; and then they put each other into ovens; and then they dropped a rather small bomb, and watched a huge cloud mushroom from it. And then, for a short while, they looked around, fearfully, for God.

Then,
A large group of people grew hard, and they started to laugh. And they laughed at themselves. And they laughed at their morality. And they laughed at hope. And they howled hysterically at love. And they giggled at filth. And then they laughed and laughed at God.
And God turned his back.
And God walked away.

The end.

# seventy-seven

The tennis ball bounces into the wrong court, and a cheerful voice calls after the grinning retriever,
"Pardon me."

Two people, each lost in his own thoughts, crowd a doorway. Each smiles deferentially to the other, murmuring,
"Pardon me."

Sitting at a counter munching on a hamburger, one reaches in front of another for the salt, saying,
"Pardon me."

One speaks a bit crudely in front of another. Looking embarrassed, he apologizes sincerely,
"Pardon me."

And one failed to retrieve a promise to God.
And one took his own way, crossing the purpose of God.

And one reached for his own will, cutting
across the God.
And one spoke crudely of God's name.

But not one said, or even thought, "Pardon
me."

God, have mercy on us.

## seventy-eight

One
Lost his job, and storming home
he snapped at his children, and
he argued with his wife,
Yet, his eyes pleaded, "Listen to me."
And no one did.

One
Lost a friend and walked the streets
And failed to speak to some whom he
    knew,
And he was rude to others,
Yet, his eyes pleaded, "Listen to me."
And no one did.

One
Lost faith in his work, his home, his faith,
And he wandered the parks and paths,
    mute
Yet, his eyes pleaded, "Listen to me."
And no one did.

And the Jesus listens past the voices, the
anger, the loneliness, and he gazes deep
into the eyes and listens.
And listens

And listens
And he waits to listen
And waits
and waits
and waits.

## seventy-nine

He saw people love each other. He saw friends love friends. He saw mothers love children. He saw husbands love wives. And he saw that all love made strenuous demands on the lovers. He saw love require sacrifice and self-denial. He saw love produce arguments and anguish. He saw it bring disappointment, pain, and even death. And he decided that it cost too much. And he decided not to diminish his life with love.

He saw people strive for distant and hazy goals. He saw men strive for success. He saw women strive for high, high ideals. He saw young people strive for attainment. And he saw that the striving was frequently mixed with disappointment. And he saw the strong men fail, maimed, and even killed. He saw it force people into pettiness, grasping at those things they both saw and didn't see. He saw that those who succeeded were sometimes those who had not earned the success. And he decided that it cost too much. He decided not to soil his life with striving.

He saw people serving others. He saw men give money to the poor and helpless. He saw whole groups work to build, cleanse, and heal others. And he saw that the more they served, the faster the need grew. He saw large portions of money freely given line already fat pockets. He saw new schools filled with uncaring teachers. He saw ungrateful receivers turn on their serving friends. And he decided that that cost too much. He decided not to soil his life with serving.

And when he died, he walked up to the God and presented him with his life. Undiminished, unmarred, and unsoiled, his life was clean from the filth of the world, and he presented it proudly to the mighty God saying, "This is my life." And the great God said,
"What life?"

## eighty

"The only thing that really counts is food," said the hungry man. "I will steal it, lie for it, and take it wherever I can. You can talk about peace and hope and everything else, but the only thing that really counts is food. Before everything else in life, man must have food in his belly." And this seemed true. The most important thing in the world is to feed and be fed.

"The only thing that really counts is happiness," said the contented man. "I've worked all my life for it. Money lets you down; ambitions tear you apart; but happiness calms you, warms you, makes life meaningful. Before everything else in life, man must have happiness. Nothing else will matter then." And this seemed true. The most important thing is to be happy and to create happiness.

"The only thing that really matters is knowledge," said the student. "I've studied all my life. All else can be taken away from you; all else can sour into self-seeking, but to learn, to know and to understand brings you closer to being fulfilled. Nothing else matters." And this seemed true. The most important thing is to learn, to know, and to understand.

And Jesus said, "I am the way, the truth, and the life." That's it. No choices. No dilemmas. No doubts. I choose Jesus. And the happy man, the hungry man, and the student look at me; and I have great compassion for them.

## eighty-one

If you're the Christ, then save yourself
They jeered up at the cross. And he didn't.
And he was the Christ.
And we were saved.

If there is a Christ, then save my daughter
A man cried from his knees. His daughter
    died.
But there is the Christ,
And the man rose and lived significantly.

If there is a Christ, then help me to succeed
A man pleaded from his knees. He failed.
But there is the Christ,
And the man lived his failure into glory.

If there is a Christ, then give me skill
A man pleaded from self-knowledge. No
    skill came.
But there is the Christ,
And the man strode to meaning without
    skill.

If there is a Christ, then give me my way
A man demanded from ambition. He was
    denied his way,
But there is the Christ,
And the man went *God's* way.

And the earth trembles.

## eighty-two

Once, on a weekday, I was spending some hours at a beach, and I saw a mother and her little boy. The day was perfect—bright and warm. The beach was quiet, and there were very few people there. In little quiet clusters they sunned and slept and read and swam lazily. All was quite different from the weekend water riot of noise, music, and shouting.

The white, white skin of both the mother and the boy told quite clearly that this was not a frequent type of outing for them. I watched the boy as he shed the tightness and duty and rigid living rules that so wrap up the life of a child today. His eyes blinked and took on the loose, mind-wandering gaze that carried him everywhere at once. I watched in delight as his whole body gave over to soaking up moments of awareness with stones, shells, and water-hardened sand ridges. He was joined by the forms of life that call and scurry in harmony with a beach. He sat and walked or squatted, idly probing with fingers and toes. Contentment covered him with a protecting shield.

Rasping, breaking the air like a rusty knife came his mother's irritated voice commanding him to go *into* the water and not to play along the beach. That's what they had come for. That's what they had sacrificed money, time, and duties for. Startled, he tried to obey, but each time the hold of imaginative minutiae halted his mind and eye and he'd slip into the world of peace. Again and again came the rusty knife. Finally, in disgust, the mother gathered up their belongings and hauling him by one wrist, she hurried him off to the too hot, too metallic car. She muttered his ungratefulness and his foolish response to the opportunity. He followed obediently, and they drove off.

And a strange grief welled in my throat. I had seen the death of peace—the gift of peace, rejected. And I prayed for the boy, and I wept for the boy, and I heard God murmur, "I know. I know."

Then I gathered up my things and went home.

# eighty-three

God laid his hand on a kneeling youth and said, "Follow me." And the youth was struck dumb. Rising from his knees, he hurried to prepare, to be worthy to serve the God, the great God who had chosen him. He went to school and worked diligently with the echo of his call burning in his ears. He knelt to meet the God, who said again, "Follow me." And he rose from his knees and, doubting his strength to serve, he set out to prepare himself physically. He trained and taught himself to do with little and to remain strong. He knelt to his God, who said once again, "Follow me." Again he rose and he studied more and continued to prepare himself in every imaginable way. For years he worked to make himself worthy of whatever task God had for him.

At long last, he felt he was ready and eagerly he knelt but he heard nothing. Looking up, he had a vision as of his looking down a long, long road. In the far distance he saw the receding figure of the God walking the road—alone. He was too far for the boy-man to try to run and catch up with. Soon he was out of sight altogether. The boy-man cursed himself and remained kneeling for a long, lonely time ... there at the beginning of the road—the road that was now swathed in darkness— and the wind whirled noiselessly about him and his loneliness.

## eighty-four

I knelt and said,
"But I am one, only one."

And the world is so large. And the evil is so strong. There are so few who care. There are so few who sense.
"But I am one, only one."

The machines of organization roll on, crushing the individual into a part of the mass. The hopelessness of the world-wrought minds spreads and smothers the hope of the lonely individuals.
"But I am one, only one."

Entire cities have been destroyed. Entire nations have reaped their seeds of distrust and lie writhing in their death throes.
"But I am one, only one."

While I eat my fill, hundreds die in hunger. While I close my door in careless safety, hundreds watch doors in fear and resignation.
"But I am one, only one."

The powers of mind and thought and measurement reduce the world to calculated probabilities.
"But I am one, only one."

And even that one walks in fear and stumbling, discontent, and lack of strength.
"And I am so one, only one."

And he said,
"Stand up,
I choose you."

And I stood up and the earth trembled,
And that is the beginning to which there
    is no end,
Except in God.

## eighty-five

Once,
Friends seemed far away and those who were near seemed unfeeling and uncaring. The job to which I was committed seemed to set off my weaknesses in sharp relief. The values which so recently had seemed dazzling now appeared, upon closer inspection, tarnished and meaningless. The world in which I lived lay deep in its own mire of deceit. My eyes swept life as I knew it, in bottomless disappointment. And so I rejected it. I decided to turn my back on this futile world and try to find life's meaning elsewhere. I stepped outside the world's fence and vowed to be blind to it for as long as I would live.

I went looking for God.

I wandered and I searched. I prayed and meditated. Unencumbered with the pulls and pains of my old world, I felt light and free; I searched for my God. I grew apprehensive, and doubt seeped in, for I could not find him.

Then,
I glanced over the fence I had so firmly re-

jected. I saw again the futile, faithless world. And there, deep in the midst of the pain stood God, talking, listening, and holding a dying child in his arms. He looked at me. I saw that to find him, to get close to him, I would have to re-enter the world I'd found so worthless. I'd have to make my way through all that I'd rejected if I were to meet my God. I felt deep anguish as I stood by the fence. His eyes were upon me, and he saw my heavy heart, and his eyes never left me.

## eighty-six

A man prayed,
"Give me strength that I might not fail."
And God gave him strength,
And he did not fail.

A woman prayed,
"Give me peace that I might face my
   world."
And he gave her peace,
And she faced her world.

A youth prayed,
"Give me wisdom that I might understand."
And he gave him wisdom,
And he understood.

An aging man prayed,
"Give me hope that my soul might not die."
And he gave him hope,
And his soul did not die.

A woman prayed,
"Give me love that I might live fully."
And he gave her love,
And she lived fully.

And a wanderer said,
"Take my mind and life that I might serve
    you."
And he took his mind and life,
And the wanderer served him.

And because of the wanderer
God smiled at the world,
And the world was bathed in the light
Of that lonely smile.

# eighty-seven

Once, a man said, "If I had some extra money, I'd give it to God, but I have just enough to support myself and my family." And the same man said, "If I had some extra time, I'd give it to God, but every minute is taken up with my job, my family, my clubs, and what have you—every single minute." And the same man said, "If I had a talent, I'd give it to God, but I have no lovely voice; I have no special skill; I've never been able to lead a group; I can't think cleverly or quickly, the way I would like to."

And God was touched,
And although it was unlike him,
God gave that man money, time, and a glorious talent.
And then he waited, and waited, and waited. . . .
Then after a while, he shrugged his shoulders,
And he took all those things right back from the man,
The money, the time, and the glorious talent.

After a while, the man sighed and said, "If I only had some of that money back, I'd give it to God. If I only had some of that time, I'd give it to God. If I could only rediscover that glorious talent, I'd give it to God."

And God said,
"Oh, shut up."

And the man told some of his friends, "You know, I'm not so sure that I believe in God anymore."

# eighty-eight

Joy
is an old-fashioned word.
What did it used to mean?

Like "happy" maybe?
Or was it "silly" and "giggly"?
Could just anyone get to it?
Or was it buried in book and brow?

I wish I knew
What it used to mean,
For I need a word,
A good, solid word.

That shows how I feel
When the day is over
And I've worked well
And I'm glad to be so tired.

I need a word for when
I've spent hours and hours
With those I love, and I'm
Talk-sore and smile-aching.

I need a word for when
I'm alone, and over the miles
Are parts of my heart, deep in others
Who are warm, and safe, and at peace.

I need a word for when
A job looms like a greyhound
And I can do it, and I want to do it
And I tingle to get at it.

I need a word for that
Warm, gentle flow that
Covers every corner of my being,
And says, "Lo I am with you always."

I need a word
Real bad,
And I think it might be
"joy"

Or maybe it's
"God."
Then again, maybe
They're the same
Word.

## eighty-nine

I know people
Who have very complete datebooks. They even have datebooks for God. And just like they arrange and fit everything into a tight, worthy schedule, they jot down appointments with God. What a satisfaction to mark solidly: time for a church meeting, or a church supper, or a special service. Now, in every busy, worthy schedule, conflicts arise. Sometimes God wins, and another item is crossed out. And then sometimes God loses—you know how it is —and he gets crossed out. It all evens out in the end, of course; in fact, in some datebooks I know, God comes out ahead.

No one seems to wonder
Whether he is in God's datebook,
Or on God's schedule.

And the Lord God formed man
And man gave names
To all cattle, and
To birds of the air
And to every beast of the field,

And he proudly named himself
"Fool"
And it all began.

# ninety

Once, I went walking with a friend. We had a goal; we knew where we were going. We walked briskly, chatted, and laughed. It began to get hot and uncomfortable. Then we got lost. Instead of irritation and frustration, however, something strange occurred to us. Our destination didn't seem to matter so much. We slowed down, at times simply meandering. At times we walked close together, discussing in earnest thoughts and feelings flowing through us. Other times, we drifted far apart, each wrapped in his own reflections, silent and musing. I remember a lot of laughter, and I remember the day dissolving, for we walked it away. I had never done that before. At long last, and purely by chance, we arrived at our initial destination, but by then we were weary and gave it only a passing examination. We went home, calm and content. I know that friend well. We've done many things together. But when I think of that friend, I don't remember the multitude of busy things we've done as much as I remember walking away a long, lazy day.

Do you suppose anyone ever comes to God in any manner other than briskly and full of business? Do people always come bristling with petty purpose? Does anyone ever meander with God, sharing fun, thoughts, and silences? Could it be that we might get more memorably close to God by being less frantic with him? Could it be that we are missing one of the loveliest potential relationships with God?

What a waste.

## ninety-one

They say
You shouldn't pray for someone's health,
for that is in the hands of his physical
makeup—his chemical balance, his envi-
ronmental pressures—and it's not fair to
blame God for those natural processes.

They say
You shouldn't pray for health or success,
for that's in the hands of chance and opportunity and ability, and it's not fair to try to
get God to intervene unfairly.

They say
You shouldn't pray for material things, for
that is selfish and immature, and it is childish to try to get God to give you a giant
handout.

They say
You should be completely composed and
spiritually recollected and lovingly tuned
in when you pray. It isn't fair to ask God
to sort through your nervous confusion.

They say
Prayer is mostly a psychic phenomenon

where, in pretended conversation, one
seeks to establish a mental equilibrium. It
isn't fair to think of a great God who will
bend way down and listen to one person's
mumblings.

I said.
"I'm lonely
I need God
            How do I pray?"
And God said,
"You just did.
Here I am."

Nuts to "they"!

## ninety-two

You know what
It is about TV?
You can turn it off,
"Click," just like that!

You know what
It is about doors?
You can close them,
"Slam," just like that!

You know what
It is about people?
You can leave them,
Turn and walk, just like that!

You know what
It is about books?
You can quit them,
Close the covers, just like that!

You know what
It is about God?
You can't do anything about him
He's there, just like that!

How do you like them apples!

# ninety-three

Once a man decided to make himself worthy for God. He knew a friend who had a deep and moving voice. He listened to him carefully, and then he trained his voice to sound just like his friend's. He knew a man who had a masterful stride. He watched him closely, and then trained himself to walk in just that way. He knew a man who had clever and profound thoughts. He spent some time with that man, and soon he had made the man's thoughts his own. He knew a man who was witty and a pleasure to be with, and he studied the man carefully, and soon he could say the same kinds of witty things, and he had the same pleasant personality.

And he stood on the curb one day.
And God walked by, and never saw him ...never even noticed him. Disappointed, the man gave up the newly trained voice and stride. He flung off the borrowed thoughts, wit and personality, and he sat down on the curb, despondent and confused.

Then
He felt a hand on his shoulder, and he
looked up to see God smiling at him. And
God said,
"Hello"
And he called him by name, and then God
said,
"Come."

## ninety-four

Out of love so deep
Love so pained
Through hope and need
He caused Man.

Out of hate so deep
Hate so pained
Through brains and skill
he created god.

Out of mind so weak
Love so blind
Through rust and memory
he sought God.

Out of mind so weak
Mind so blind
Through refinement and skill
he killed god.

Out of void so bleak
Void so pained
Through decay and rot
he destroyed he.

## ninety-five

Once upon a time
There was the beginning of a man
Who grew in wisdom and stature
While the needy world waited.

In between two tasks
He took a journey on a train
And found lovely, undisturbed peace,
Not being anywhere, but rushing on.

His mind loosed its bounds
Dozing and dancing, while his eyes
Gazed unseeing at the undefined blurs
Streaming by his private window.

When the train did stop
A mute, uniformed conductor
Gathered the bags and offered an arm
To help him bridge the step.

The man hesitated,
Looked a chasmed moment
At buildings now solidly marked
Filled with faces, bricks, and tears.

Turning quickly back
He reboarded his train

Found his seat and lunged into it
In order to ride "one more stop."

It's ten years since then
And still he rides that train
And still he looks out his window
At the gentle, floating world.

Unsought and serene
He displays a tireless, childish smile
To the gutted world, the lifeless faces
Fixed for the moment at each train stop.
God, have mercy on us.

## ninety-six

Today I experienced fear, real fear.
One came to me and sat across from me and talked and talked and poured out his mind and heart. He is rejecting the faith of his childhood, of his family, of his heritage, and he is doing so after painful, careful, sincere thought. Growing bitter and resentful, he calmly damned all organized religion. His examples were clear, pertinent, and too often had the smack of truth.

Having had years of training in a faith, he wanders now in search of a solitary belief that will provide a meaning for a new set of values. His one sure conviction at this point is that wherever the answer is, it isn't going to be in any religion as we know it today.

I am convinced he will search and find some sort of values. I am equally convinced that his rejected faith is providing him with the need and a frame of reference for these values, whether he recognizes it or not.

I asked him if he would train his children in a religion. And he replied, "No." I asked him where they would get their need and their frame of reference for a set of values. He looked past me, out of the window and said softly several times, "I don't know. I don't know."

We talked gently on and on until it had
  grown dark outside,
And I felt fear,
Real fear.

God have mercy on us.

## ninety-seven

I    There was a man who had a friend, and his friend needed help, and he helped his friend, but it wasn't enough and he walked away from his friend sorrowing and mumbling "not good enough." And he turned to his job, and saw what needed to be done, and he worked at the job, but it was not done well, and someone else had to finish it, and the man walked away sorrowing and mumbling, "not good enough." And the man had a vision of the way he would like to be, and he worked at that vision, and he strove for that vision, and he only half fit that vision, ever, and he walked away mumbling and sorrowing, "not good enough." *Ever-striving attitude*

And the great God
Interrupted his mumbling and sorrowing,
He said, "Come."

II    There was a man who was a good friend, when he had time, and he frequently said to himself, "I'm as good a friend as most, and better than some." The man did his job, and did it pretty well, and was as honest as most and more honest than some. And the man built his life so it would fit the demands of the world, his family, his business and church, and it was as good as most and better than some.

*Complacent Attitute*

And the great God
Shrugged his shoulders, and
He said, "not good enough."

## ninety-eight

"You, therefore, must be perfect, as your heavenly Father is perfect."

I've heard people moan about the trick the Christ had played on them, asking them to strive toward an impossible goal. I've heard the atheist sneer, "Show me just *one* true Christian!" And I couldn't. I've listened to sincere, striving Christians grow despondent as they acknowledged their failure to measure up to Christ's command.

I've had the long, dull moments aching with the realization that though each day I start fresh, each evening I reflect on the unmet, unseen, and unresponded to challenges.

But then, I've also felt the smile of Christ as I attempted what he said, and it has drowned out his sighs of disappointment in me. I've felt the glow of God permeate my every pore as I finally woke up to his direction in me, and it smothered his soul-stinging waves of disappointment at other times.

I can't wipe out the doubts and fears in my self-knowledge of not measuring up. But I can walk each day seeking to

174

fulfill what he wants in me. I may not achieve hours of grace, but I can achieve the moments of gentle approval.

And those moments are the meaning of life.

# ninety-nine

Feeling blue?
Buy some clothes.
Feeling lonely?
Turn on the radio.
Feeling despondent?
Read a funny book.
Feeling bored?
Watch TV
Feeling empty?
Eat a sundae,
Feeling worthless?
Clean the house.
Feeling sad?
Tell a joke.

Ain't this modern age wonderful?
You don't gotta feel nothin',
There's a substitute for everythin'!

God have mercy on us.